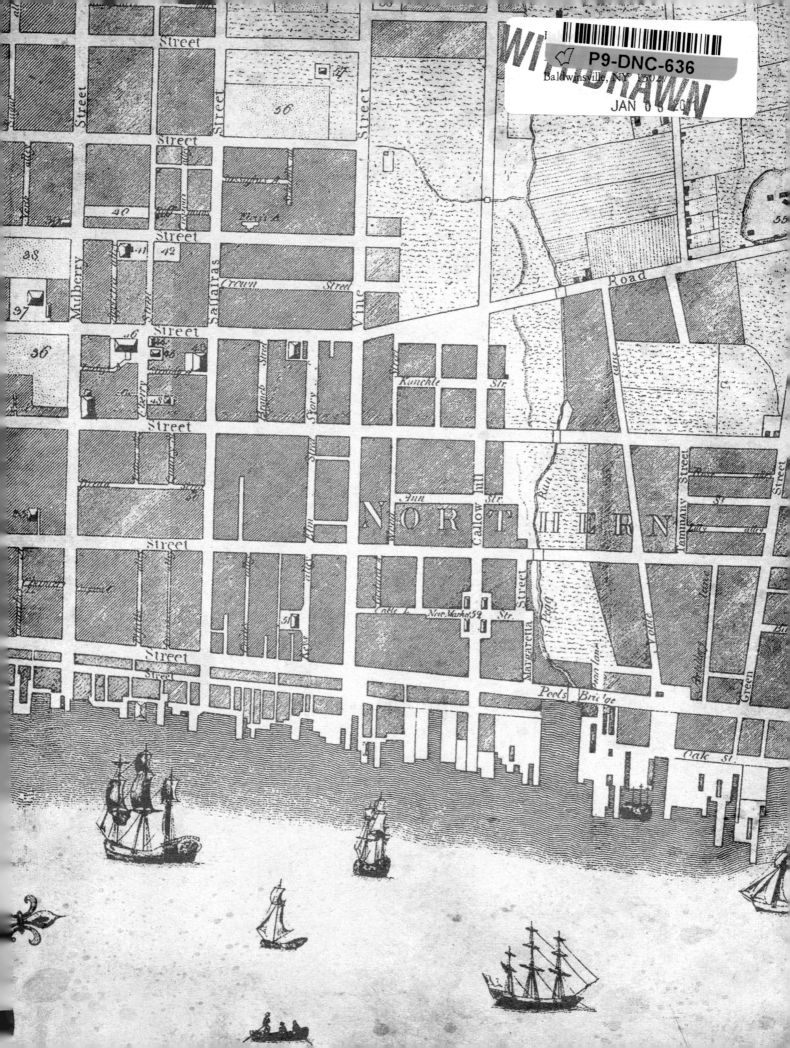

A FEAST of FREEDOM

TASTY TIDBITS FROM
THE CITY TAVERN

WALTER STAIB
AND JENNIFER FOX

ILLUSTRATED BY FERNANDO JUAREZ

RP|KIDS

For my children,
Patrick and Elizabeth

9 8 7 6 5 4 3 2 1
Digit on the right indicates the number of this printing.

Library of Congress Control Number: 2009936574

ISBN 978-0-7624-3598-2

Cover and interior design by Frances J. Soo Ping Chow
Typography: Copperplate, Gill Sans, ITC Berkeley, Stockton, and Swinging

Published by Running Press Kids,
an imprint of Running Press Book Publishers
2300 Chestnut Street
Philadelphia, PA 19103-4371

Visit us on the web!
www.runningpress.com
www.citytavern.com

FOREWORD

The late 1700s were a time of great change in America. Tired of being taxed and told what to do by a king who lived thousands of miles away, the original thirteen colonies started to break away from their mother country, England. The colonists pushing for freedom were an altogether new breed of men (...and ladies...and children), and America itself was an entirely new sort of place. Free from stuffy traditions, Americans had fresh ideas and new ways of thinking. They dreamed of a country where leaders were chosen by the people, all men were created equal, and citizens were free to think for themselves about whatever they wanted—be it art, science, politics, or what sort of wig to wear.

The city at the heart of colonial America was Philadelphia, Pennsylvania—the hub of American culture, politics, and society. And the heart of any colonial city worth its salt was a tavern, a place to eat meals, chat with friends, catch up on current events...or *even* plan a revolution. Philadelphia was no exception. It boasted one of the greatest taverns of the day, and one that would become forever tied to the birth of our nation.

This is the story of Philadelphia's historic City Tavern.

Well...come along now. Turn the page. I haven't got all day. I was born in 1770. I'm not getting any younger!

A TAVERN IS BORN

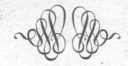

In 1770, a group of fifty-three fine gentlemen from Philadelphia came together with a common purpose. They needed a fashionable place to meet friends, do business, discuss politics, play cards, or simply share a tasty meal. The local inns and taverns of the time just didn't cut the mustard. Pooling their money, the men decided to create their own tavern. They would each become founding members and pay a fee to join.

The men hired an architect from London to create the new meeting place, and in 1773, the City Tavern was open for business. Based on the very best taverns in England, it quickly became one of the finest in the New World. The Tavern earned the praise of many notable men of the day, including Founding Father John Adams who described the Tavern as "the most genteel one in America."

THE TAVERN TOP-TO-BOTTOM

ATTIC: A small attic on the very top floor was used as servants' quarters for Tavern workers.

THIRD FLOOR: The Tavern's third floor contained lodging rooms, where guests could stay overnight. Often as many as fifty men or more would crowd into the few rooms, sleeping six or seven to a bed. Close quarters indeed!

SECOND FLOOR: The second floor was home to the Long Room, the Tavern's grand ballroom and dining space. This floor also contained two private dining rooms, the Northwest Dining Room and the Charter Room, which was reserved for use by founding members of the Tavern.

FIRST FLOOR: The main entrance to the Tavern featured a marble staircase from the street level, leading up to the first floor of the building. This floor contained the Subscription, Coffee, and Bar Rooms, as well as access to the back garden and outhouse.

CELLAR LEVEL: The cellar level was used exclusively by staff and contained areas for some food storage and preparation. A main pantry room was equipped with its own running water and bell system. These features were extremely unique for the time and aided staff in the preparation of room service for lodgers at the Tavern. Because most cooking in this period was done by fire—too smoky and unsafe to occur indoors— the main cooking would be done in outdoor smokehouses in the area behind the Tavern.

LOCATION, LOCATION, LOCATION

A key to the City Tavern's success was its location. Just blocks from the Delaware River, a major route for travel and trade ships, the Tavern was one of the first stops for visitors and seafaring merchants. In these early days, long before telephones, e-mail, airplanes, and the Internet—news, people, and products traveled much more slowly.

Ship captains at the time, were like traveling salesmen bringing news from other countries and selling their cargo wherever they went for whatever price they could command. A captain might load his hulls with Valencia oranges in Spain, paying ten cents a dozen. In the New World, where they had limited access to goods or the knowledge of their prices abroad, he might charge five times that much—or fifty cents a dozen—earning himself a hefty profit. Along the way, he would also exchange news between Europe and the New World. In its choice spot by the Delaware, the City Tavern became a bustling place for the exchange of the latest news and goods.

FEAST
OF FLAVORS

While the colonists did not have such modern delicacies as frozen chicken nuggets and pizza bagels, the food served at fine establishments such as City Tavern was *far* from boring. Thanks to the location of the nearby port, the cuisine was a truly delectable melting pot of foodstuffs from all around the globe. There were exotic fruits, spices, and peppers from the West Indies, hearty sausages and baked goods from Germany, traditional stews and meat pies from England, and fine cheeses and wine from France. An abundance of local fish, game, and produce (such as corn, squash, berries, and beans first cultivated by Native Americans) blended with foreign flavors to create a cuisine as new and unique as America itself.

The fashionable dinner hour of the day was 4:00 PM, and meals were served family style, where large platters and tureens of the dishes of the day were brought to the table for sharing. Courses were divided into: *first plates*—a selection of salads, appetizers, and soups; *second plates*—or main courses, typically meat dishes; and *desserts*—cakes, cobblers, puddings, and pies. A feast for a large group might last three or four hours and contain up to twenty different dishes per course, requiring a healthy appetite and expandable breeches.

HAVING A BALL!

The main dining and party room at the Tavern was known as the Long Room. This was where all the action happened—balls, banquets, meetings, card games, and concerts. And, it was *indeed* a very long room, considered the second largest ballroom in the country at that time after the one in nearby Independence Hall.

Balls in the City Tavern were a magnificent affair. Well-to-do ladies and gentlemen would dress in their finest to enjoy an opulent evening of dancing and socializing. There were numerous amusements ranging from puppet shows to fortune-tellers, jugglers to musicians, and huge tables were laden with food. Of course, it was considered improper for women in the eighteenth century to eat in public, so should a lady wish to dine she would have to use one of the smaller guest rooms upstairs.

FOOD FOR THOUGHT

The City Tavern was not simply a place for lavish dinners and parties. Within its walls one could also engage in intellectual pursuits such as reading. In fact, there was an entire room dedicated to just that. The Subscription Room was filled with magazines and newspapers from around the globe. Colonists wishing to stay abreast of the latest news could spend hours pouring over the Tavern's impressive collection of periodicals.

A particularly popular paper at the Tavern was the *Pennsylvania Gazette*, a newspaper published by local printer and all-around colonial superstar, Benjamin Franklin. An American original, Franklin was—among other things—an author, diplomat, inventor, scientist, and statesman. He even found time to help discover electricity and establish the postal service. Especially loved for his sharp mind and quick wit, Franklin infused his newspaper with humor and creativity, making it the best-known in all of the colonies and the first to feature a cartoon.

English, quite refined. Smooth finish.

A JOLT OF JAVA

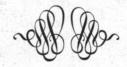

Before or after a good read, patrons might be tempted to indulge in a steaming hot cuppa joe, *coffee* that is. The potent black brew was introduced in the colonies in the late 1600s, and by the mid-1700s, it was just as popular as tea. Like taverns, colonial coffee houses were places for gentlemen to socialize and share ideas about business and politics. Many taverns, the City Tavern included, doubled as coffee houses, and the name "Coffee House" was often used to refer to taverns.

The Coffee Room at City Tavern did not simply serve coffee, it was also headquarters to the Merchants' Coffee House and Place of Exchange. Here merchants, ship's captains, and other businessmen gathered to trade goods, including coffee, and shared shipping import and export news.

TROUBLE BREWING

Coffee wasn't the only thing causing a stir by the late eighteenth century. In December of 1773, colonists in Massachusetts, dressed as Native Americans, dumped more than three hundred chests of tea from three ships into Boston Harbor. They had not lost their minds nor gotten very, very thirsty. Instead, they were protesting a tax the king had placed on tea by destroying large quantities of the stuff. This little incident—which further boosted the popularity of coffee in the New World—became known as the Boston Tea Party.

The king, who was rather used to being in charge, did not take kindly to the colonists' rebellious behavior. Five months later, he punished the wayward citizens of Massachusetts. He banned town meetings, required colonists to house British troops, and worst of all closed Boston Harbor, one of the colonies' largest ports of trade. In May 1774, Paul Revere—a fellow from Massachusetts known for riding around on his horse and shouting—arrived at the City Tavern spreading word that Boston Harbor had been shut down. Revere hoped to rally support for Massachusetts and knew the Tavern was just the place to do it.

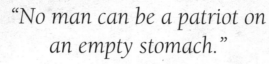

*"No man can be a patriot on
an empty stomach."*
—William Cowper Brann

When colonists at the Tavern heard Revere's news they were outraged. A group of fifty-five delegates from twelve different colonies gathered in Philadelphia to discuss the matter. Known as the First Continental Congress, the group's official meeting place was Carpenters' Hall. The functional room where they met served its purpose just fine. However, the delegates soon discovered that solving the problems of an entire nation made them rather hungry and thirsty. Conveniently, the City Tavern, was located nearby. The Tavern soon became the Congress's main hangout. It was *the* place to go to finish up the day's business or gossip about the latest news in a civilized manner—over a meal and a glass of wine. It's been said that more business was conducted in the evenings in the Tavern's Long Room than during the official sessions at Carpenters' Hall.

As a result of the meetings, the king's harsh restrictions became known as the "Intolerable Acts." And the First Continental Congress responded to the acts by drafting a letter stating the colonies' rights and threatening to cease trade with England. This response would go unanswered by the angry king and become a first big step on America's road to independence.

LET FREEDOM RING

The relationship between the colonists and the king continued to sour. In April of 1775, British troops fired on a group of Americans in Lexington, Massachusetts, killing eight men. With these shots, the Revolutionary War between England and America had begun! Delegates of the Second Continental Congress met in Philadelphia. In June, they decided to create an army, and John Adams nominated George Washington as its commander. The motion was quickly accepted.

By 1776, the colonists decided it was about time to declare their independence from England. Thomas Jefferson, a scholar and statesman known for his writing skill, was chosen by the Congress to draft the Declaration of Independence. Working tirelessly, and taking his meals at the City Tavern, Jefferson completed the document in just a little over two weeks. The Declaration was officially adopted on July 4, 1776, which became, as John Adams noted, "the anniversary of American Independence." A year later, on July 4, 1777, the very first Independence Day celebration was held at the City Tavern. It was a spectacle like Philadelphia had never seen. Candles lit up every window in the Tavern, and a thirteen-gun salute rang out through the air. There were also parades, fireworks, a naval review in the nearby Delaware River, and of course, a wonderful meal attended by some of the greatest patriots in American history. (And one or two not so great ones.)

HEADQUARTERS FOR THE BIG CHEESE

Soon after the Fourth of July banquet, news reached Philadelphia that the British were planning to take the city. General Washington had to act. He moved into Philadelphia in August and made the Tavern a temporary headquarters. The city allowed Washington the best possible modes of communication as he tried to monitor the movements of British General Howe and his fleet of ships.

During this time at the Tavern, Washington had a private dinner with a young French officer, the Marquis de Lafayette. Spurred by his belief in the colonists' cause and his own daring sense of adventure, Lafayette was a wealthy Frenchman who came to America to join the war effort. He had just been commissioned by Congress as a major general in the army. Washington and Lafayette got along swimmingly, and their dinner at City Tavern blossomed into a lifelong friendship, as well as a key alliance in the war. Lafayette served as one of Washington's best officers and helped gain France's support for America.

Liberty for All!
Vive la France!

THE BRITISH ARE CO-HERE!!

Geneneral Washington left Philadelphia later that month. The British fleet had moved out, and the city was safe. Well, *not exactly*. Howe and his ships had simply regrouped and entered the city from a different point. By September of 1777, the British occupied Philadelphia, including the beloved City Tavern. While many Philadelphians were gravely disheartened by this turn of events, one was not—the tavern-keeper Daniel Smith. Though he had happily organized the City Tavern's foremost patriotic celebrations of the day—including the extravagant Independence Day bash—at heart Smith remained loyal to England. So when British officers took over the Tavern, Smith welcomed them with open arms...and kitchen...and bar.

Unlike Washington's troops who'd stayed away from the temptations of the city, the British soldiers were more than happy to indulge in every delight and amusement on offer. The Tavern—once a scene of genteel debate and upper-crust soirées—became a den of drinking, partying, and gambling. But the fun wouldn't last. In no time, the whole city was depleted of food, drink, and other necessities. The British troops' behavior became *so* bad that their officers had to turn the Tavern into a makeshift prison, holding trials for their own soldiers. With nothing left to gain from the occupation but trouble, the British decided to move along, taking Daniel Smith with them.

A NEW DAY

The departure of Daniel Smith and the end of the war marked the dawn of a new era for the City Tavern, Philadelphia, and America. In October of 1781, British General Charles Cornwallis surrendered at Yorktown, Virginia. Two years later the Treaty of Paris was signed, officially ending the war and acknowledging America's independence from England. The new country crackled with the buzz of freedom and hope. And no place more so than Philadelphia. People gathered to celebrate and bid good-bye to wartime friends. Under new management, the Tavern hosted scores of patriotic dinners and balls.

The colonists were now free to make their own choices and rules, and America was its own nation. But with this freedom also came responsibility and a slew of new problems. Used to relying on England for rules and resources, the new nation had to start from scratch—establishing trade relationships, ways to settle disputes, and means of governing themselves. Like many businesses, the City Tavern struggled to find its way in the changing climate of the new country.

WE THE PEOPLE...

It soon became clear that America needed to establish a formal set of rules and regulations for how it was to be run. So in May of 1787, a group of fifty-five delegates from every state except Rhode Island, who did not wish to participate, gathered in Philadelphia to create such a document. Known as the "Philadelphia Convention," and later the "Constitutional Convention," the members included several prominent leaders such as Benjamin Franklin, Alexander Hamilton, and James Madison, who took copious notes and was considered the "Father of the Constitution." Ever-popular George Washington, a delegate from Virginia, was elected by his peers to be the president of the convention.

Framing the rules for an entire country was a very large and difficult job. Arguments broke out and compromises had to be reached. Many evenings were spent at the City Tavern with small groups of delegates planning and plotting in hushed tones. After much fussing and fighting, the convention come together to create the United States Constitution, outlining the framework of the country's government. Beginning, "We the People of the United States...", the document stressed the power of the people to govern themselves. Fearing another king, power was divided between three branches of government, one of which would be a leader or president. (Ultimately, the job would fall to George Washington.) The convention celebrated a job well done with a big blowout at the Tavern.

WASHINGTON ON HIS WAY

In April 1789, the City Tavern held a banquet for George Washington on his way to New York City (the nation's capital at the time) to become America's first president. This was not the first banquet at the Tavern to honor Mr. Washington. Over the years, there had been many others, including a particularly poignant event less than six years earlier celebrating a much different purpose—Washington's retirement from public life. After saying his heartfelt good-byes to friends and colleagues after the war, Washington returned to his home at Mount Vernon in Virginia to live out the rest of his years quietly. However, he soon discovered the nation had very different plans for him—namely, running the country.

Returning to Philadelphia in 1789, Washington was greeted as a hero. Enormous crowds cheered him in the street, and his pre-inauguration dinner at the City Tavern was a grand and elegant affair. The festivities, including a dinner for two hundred and fifty guests in the Long Room, music, dancing, and a display of fireworks, lasted long into the night, with the guests' spirits buoyed by the hope of things to come.

And as the last fireworks faded, the air filled with a sense of calm. This new country, once merely a dream of men sharing ideas within the walls of a tavern, was now a reality. Though no one knew what tomorrow would bring, everyone was filled with the promise of things to come.

And the rest, as they say, is *history*.

OTHER TASTY TIDBITS...

- Some say the City Tavern may be haunted. People at the Tavern have reported feeling cold blasts of air when no windows or doors were opened and finding place settings on tables completely rearranged when no one is around. So who's the ghost? Rumor has it, a waiter was killed by a patron with a sword on a particularly rowdy night in the 1700s.

- Most people know that a bar is a place that serves drinks. But do you know where the term came from? The place where you got a drink used to be called a "dispensary." If patrons got too wild, the staff would lower a grate of bars down for protection. In time, the dispensary became known as simply the bar.

- The City Tavern didn't just sell food and drink, it also sold tickets. Early accounts show that patrons could purchase tickets to special events at local venues, such as concerts or Shakespeare plays.

- Because there was no indoor plumbing during the heyday of the City Tavern, patrons who needed the restroom would have to excuse themselves and head outdoors to the outhouse.

- If you go to a restaurant today, you might see a sign saying "NO DOGS ALLOWED." But back in the day, it was not unusual to see dogs in the City Tavern, lounging under the tables or begging for scraps from their masters. In fact, you might see other animals, such as chickens, roaming the premises, too!

OLD-FASHIONED CORN BREAD*

To Europeans, "corn" has always been a generic name for all grains, and "maize," from the American Indian *mahiz*, has referred specifically to what Americans know as corn. The colonists associated this native grain not only with the New World but also with the Indians who introduced them to it; they, therefore, referred to the grain frequently as "Indian corn" to differentiate it from other varieties.

Not only was corn bread included in period cookbooks, but related corn recipes appeared frequently as well, including baked and boiled Indian pudding, mush, and Johny or Johnny cakes, also known as journey and hoe cakes. These mildly sweet (if they were sweetened at all) dishes called for cornmeal, whole corn, or even, as in the case of Thomas Jefferson's "Corn Pudding" recipe, green (unripened) corn.

Like this version of cornbread, these recipes were flavorful and quick to prepare. In addition, as they were frequently served alongside European-inspired dishes on eighteenth-century dining tables, corn bread and its related preparations certainly represented distinctively American foodways.

SERVES 10 TO 12

2 cups coarse yellow cornmeal
2 cups all-purpose flour
½ cup sugar
2 tablespoons baking powder
1 teaspoon salt
2 cups whole milk
¼ pound lard or margarine
2 large eggs, lightly beaten

1. Preheat the oven to 400°F. Grease two 8½ x 4½ x 2½ loaf pans with butter.

2. In a large mixing bowl, add the cornmeal, flour, sugar, baking powder, and salt; stir to combine.

3. In a medium-size mixing bowl, combine the milk, lard, and eggs. Add to the dry ingredients, and stir until just moistened.

4. Pour the batter into the prepared pans. Bake for 30 to 35 minutes, or until golden brown and a toothpick inserted in the center comes out clean.

5. Cool in the pan for 30 minutes to prevent crumbling.

* from *City Tavern: Recipes from the Birthplace of American Cuisine*

Time Line of Historic Events

DECEMBER 1773: The City Tavern opens for business.

MAY 1774: Paul Revere arrives to announce the closing of the port of Boston, England's response to the Boston Tea Party five months earlier.

SEPTEMBER TO OCTOBER 1774: The First Continental Congress meets in Philadelphia to respond to the Intolerable Acts. The City Tavern becomes the delegates' unofficial meeting place as they discuss business while taking their meals at the Tavern.

APRIL 1775: The Revolutionary War begins when the first shots are fired in Lexington, Massachusetts.

JUNE 1775: The Second Continental Congress appoints George Washington to lead the colonial army.

JULY 1776: The Declaration of Independence, written by Thomas Jefferson, is adopted by the Continental Congress. (While writing the Declaration, Jefferson ate most of his meals at the Tavern.)

JULY 1777: The nation's first Fourth of July celebration is held at the City Tavern.

AUGUST 1777: George Washington moves his headquarters to the Tavern, where he also meets and dines with Lafayette.

SEPTEMBER 1777: British soldiers occupy Philadelphia and the City Tavern.

FEBRUARY 1778: France officially becomes an American ally in the war.

OCTOBER 1781: The British surrender at Yorktown, Virginia.

SEPTEMBER 1783: The Treaty of Paris is signed by England and America, marking the official end of the war and American independence.

DECEMBER 1783: The Tavern hosts George Washington's retirement banquet.

SEPTEMBER 1787: The U.S. Constitution is ratified.

APRIL 1789: An inauguration banquet is held at the Tavern for George Washington on his way to being sworn in as the first president of the United States of America.

THE TAVERN TODAY

Heavily damaged by fire in 1834, the same year that the Merchant Exchange moved to another building, the City Tavern was demolished in 1854. As part of Philadelphia's bicentennial celebration, the National Park Service rebuilt the Tavern in 1975 and re-opened it for business in 1976.

Today, the Tavern is run by Chef Walter Staib, who takes great pride in transporting visitors back in time for an authentic taste of tavern life. Chef Staib makes sure every detail—from delicious colonial recipes to Prussian blue paint on the walls (a favorite of George Washington's)—are just as they should be. The City Tavern is open to patrons 365 days a year, with the exception of a few days each year for general maintenance. It has played host to several notable modern-day Americans including President Bill Clinton, former secretaries of state Henry Kissinger, George Schultz, and Alexander Haig, Senator Edward Kennedy and his entire extended family, and author David McCullough. In December 2008, City Tavern hosted the opening dinner of the National Governors Association coordinated by former Philadelphia mayor and current Pennsylvania Governor Edward G. Rendell along with then President-Elect Barack Obama before his address in Philadelphia.

City Tavern